20 Ways to Fail in Business

How to Avoid the Pitfalls
of Everyday Business Management

By Carl Powell III

I0473547

As an entrepreneur that has worked at businesses for 40 years, I have had my share of failures. Each time I failed, I looked to see what it was that caused me to fail. Each time, I found some little "nugget" that I could take with me to help me avoid failure in the next effort. This book is made up of a number of the lessons I learned during all this time in business. In each case, I'll mention the problem and what I now see as the solution to that "killer." My hope is that you'll avoid these pitfalls and be more successful as a result.

Table of Contents

20 Ways to Fail in Business

By Carl Powell III

Introduction

Just because I know *how* to fail at business, it does not necessarily mean that I am a failure at business myself. I'm an entrepreneur. I think I have always been an entrepreneur. The idea of making or obtaining something and selling it to someone else in a way that makes them happy and makes me money is something I've been utilizing since elementary school. I have tried in more than a hundred ways to make money and help people. Some worked quite well, some not so well. Some lasted a while, others only a few days. Some never got off the ground.

Each and every time I tried something, I have been able to look back and analyze that situation and learn from it. I don't know why, but I have been blessed with a fantastic memory of the past. Not an eidetic or photographic memory, just a good memory of things said, actions taken, interactions with people, and a lot of visual memories. It is a blessing to be able to look back at these times and think about every move, every nuance, every person involved, and try to see why things worked out or didn't work out. These are the lessons I've learned from all these efforts.

These are not made up stories. Each of these things actually happened and I'm relaying them to you as closely as I can without exposing anyone else in the process. You may find yourself asking how so many things could have happened to one person trying to find the right business. But I will tell you a couple of the things that kept me trying: *I don't give up easily, and I don't waste a lot of time once I realize a business venture is not going to make it.*

By reading this book, it is my belief that if you avoid all the pitfalls that are listed here, you will be able to be successful in the business you choose. Of course there no guarantees and your success will still depend on what you choose and how hard you work. But these guidelines of what NOT to do will keep you from making a lot of mistakes.

Although I have "failed" at many attempts in business, I do not consider myself a failure. I consider myself to be "moderately successful" at the least. Others consider me to be very successful. I've been self-employed and operating the same business for well over 20 years. That says a lot about my success. About half of all new businesses don't make it past the fourth year. I'm proud of what I have been able to accomplish.

But just as important as my successes have been my failures or near failures, because I learned from each of them. And those lessons have been some of the best of my life.

The earlier lessons were short and sweet, and so will be their stories. Others were deeper stories with many facets and longer narratives. But all are important.

Chapter 1
Limit Yourself to Just One Customer

One of the earliest attempts at selling for me was back in elementary school at Blake Elementary in Sheffield, AL. I was in the fourth or fifth grade and still learning to fit in like everyone else in school there. I can remember even then, that some of the boys would toss pennies against the wall before school and the closest one would win the others. This was not a school in a mid-city neighborhood full of high-rise apartment buildings. This was a one-story school in the middle of a southern small town with lots of little houses surrounding it. But even there, kids found out how to play games in the hopes of getting more than they invested. But that type of income did not appeal to me. I knew the chances of success were small and unpredictable.

That Christmas, my brothers and I got a new Mattel ThingMaker™ that made Creepy Crawlers™. It came with Gobbledygoop™ that you squeezed into molds and then cooked until they solidified. After it cooked, you used a special handle to move the mold into a water bath so it would cool enough to touch. Then you could remove the rubbery little insects and worms to play with, trade, and later (with special Gobbledygook) eat!

I began to take some of these to school and show them to my friends. They were fascinating to all and it made me feel popular for a few seconds. One girl in my class in particular was enamored with them and she had a little extra money in her pocket. So, she offered me a nickel for one of them. And I thought about it and accepted it. WOW! My first sale! That felt really cool!

So, I showed her some more and she bought a couple more. The next day, I brought more and showed them to her. I think she kept buying from me until she felt she had all she needed. Then, I looked around to see who else might want to buy them. The problem was, she seemed to be the only one interested. No matter how many ways, or how many colors I put in them, she had reached what we in economics call "the law of diminishing returns." Sales to her had reached "saturation" – she no longer had interest in my products.

Of course, looking back, there were lots of things I could have done about the situation. I could have "advertised" by telling everyone in all the classes that I had these great little creatures for sale, or had my friends tell them. Or, I could have asked my one customer for a referral, someone else she thought may have been a good prospect. But the truth was, I had no idea what these concepts were or how to proceed. So, my first business venture, selling Creepy Crawlers, had to close. Although not a total failure, it was not a shining success either. But I'll never forget that it got me started into the world of selling and making a profit.

When you consider a business, you really need to ask yourself "how many customers are out there?" Seeing a single customer, no matter how good a customer they may be, is not enough to base your business on it. Even if that one customer tells you they can buy all you can make or obtain, don't settle for one customer. You simply can't base a business on a single customer. If you do, your entire business relies upon their decision to continue to do business with you. All they would have to do is change their mind about their source, or stop selling your product and you would have to close.

You need a lot of customers to support a business. When you get down to just a few, regardless of how important those customers are, you have placed yourself in danger and you really need to expand.

Chapter 2
Make Sure to Have Limited Materials Available

In my first real economics class in college, we began to discuss the basics of Supply and Demand. Anyone who has ever had an economics class should know about these basics. However, I had gone to a small private school that had to get by with the instructors they had available. I think they drew straws and the one who taught my class got the short straw. We spent most of the time reading articles from magazines and doing reports on them. I had never heard about Supply and Demand when I got to college. But I had experienced it.

Not long after my first sales experience with the Creepy Crawlers, I found my next opportunity. In the 1960's, Alabama still offered a deposit on glass soda bottles that were returned to the stores. These were the heavy-duty glass bottles that were reused after being washed and sterilized. Some states still offer these return deposits to help reduce trash and for recycling purposes. At the time, a single bottle deposit was somewhere between three and five cents. So, I started with the bottles at my house.

"Can I have these, Mom?" That's where I started. I would put them in the basket on my bicycle and head for the local convenience store. (At the time, we just called them neighborhood markets, but *sans* gas pumps, they were about the same.) When I arrived, I would bring them in, let the owner count them, and take them to the back where they would await pickup from the local soda distributors. In exchange, I received cold, hard, cash for these little babies!

In the 1960's, once a young boy got more than 25 or 30 cents in his hands, he was rich! (We could go to a Saturday morning matinee at the movie for 10-15¢, so that was a lot of money.) I can still remember the rows and rows of candy, gum, small toys, snacks and other goodies just waiting on me to pick them. I could study those shelves for a long time figuring out how to get the most for my money. A full sized candy bar was only 5-10¢, and there were lots of gum, jawbreakers, Atomic Fireballs™, and other candies for 1¢ each as well. I soon learned to calculate the total even with taxes.

Our tax rate at that time was only 4%, so I also learned that if I kept my single purchases below 25¢, I could avoid having to pay taxes. I know Jack, the owner, got really tired of me spending 24¢ at a time over and over. But soon, the small amount of change I received was all spent, my pockets were full as well as my mouth, and it was time to go back into the world to seek my fortune again.

Since the bottles were gone from the house, I had to expand my search. I'm pretty sure I asked a few of the neighbors if they had any they didn't want, but everyone knew they represented cash, so I got few takers. Then, I remembered seeing a bottle on the side of the road and went searching for it and more.

A little background here... Litter has always been a problem. However, the anti-litter campaigns didn't start until the 1950's, and even then, were an attempt to misdirect us from the real problem: The manufacturing of non-reusable containers that could fill the world with trash. So, in the 1960's, it was not unusual to see areas of our roads covered in small trash, bottles, cups, bags and more. I have spent a lot of time looking through that kind of trash as I walked trying to find a diamond in the dump, so to speak.

With that kind of trash around, there were lots of places near my house where motorists tossed things out their windows. Among the trash were some of these soda bottles that were like those little diamonds to me. I began to spend my Saturday mornings riding and searching. I would look in the edges of the woods near the road, in drainage ditches, and anywhere else I thought someone might toss one of these little goodies. Some of the bottles I took into the store were nearly unrecognizable due to the mud and grossness on and inside the bottles. And often, the manager had to check to make sure they actually took the brand of soda that the bottle represented.

But I continued until I started having a hard time finding bottles. Oh, sure, I would find an occasional bottle, but the large numbers had become smaller and smaller numbers until, finally, I had a hard time finding any at all. People just weren't throwing them out fast enough! (Tongue in cheek, of course.)

Maybe it was because people had begun to have a conscience about littering because of the TV commercials warning us of the horrible things awaiting us if we didn't stop. Maybe I just didn't expand my search area enough. Whatever the reason, my supply had dried up.

In this case, the normal rules of Supply and Demand didn't hold true. Normally, a smaller supply would drive the price up. But in this case, I had constant demand since they would buy all I brought as a matter of requirement. Still, with no supply, there was no profit. I didn't mind working for a living, (even at 10 years old), but I had nowhere else to turn. My supply was just too limited to support an ongoing business.

You are now just a couple of chapters into this book, but do not be confused by these little stories. They have real meaning and actually apply to any business. You cannot expect any business (that you believe to have any reasonable amount of demand) to be successful unless you have a good supply of goods and/or services to provide.

Chapter 3
Take Your Cut Off of the Top

During my elementary school years, we began to get active in Cub Scouts and later Boy Scouts. One of the things I enjoyed about both organizations was my subscription to Boy's Life magazine. It was filled with interesting stories and wonderful advertisements. Near the back of the magazine, there were lots of moneymaking opportunities for the adventurous and energetic scout.

One such ad was for Grit Newspaper like the one above. In fact, if you cut that kid's hair a little shorter and add about 10-15 pounds to him, it could have been me! Some really smart people on Madison Avenue created the advertisements. And although they look simplistic by today's standards, those prizes looked like gold statues to a scout with an overactive imagination. Free Prizes AND up to $2.00 to **$10 EVERY WEEK!?!??** I could not wait to get started!

Somehow, I convinced my parents that this was the right job for me. I could sell them door-to-door each week after school and I could make money off every one I sold. This ad was a little later because when I sold it, the price was 15¢ per copy and 5¢ from every copy was "mine to keep." We ordered my first supply and I started counting up the profits as I waited for them.

When the newspapers arrived, I got busy right away going door-to-door selling the Grit! Some bought because it was cute to see a little pudgy kid selling a family newspaper door to door. A few bought because they wanted to reward me for my efforts (I do that to this day with kids that sell door to door). But most just said, "No, thank you." Then sent me on my way.

I don't remember how many weeks this lasted, perhaps a few, maybe as many as four or five. But each week, my zeal subsided a little and it got harder and harder to sell. I tried selling at church one evening out in front after services and got a lesson from one of the members about "moneychangers at the Temple" which really embarrassed me.

Here's how the program worked: You tell the company how many copies you want each week. They ship them to you, you sell them, then send them the money for the total number you received. If you didn't order enough copies, you would be ok. You'd just have to order more next week. If you got too many, and didn't sell them all, you still had to pay for them. Outdated newspapers have no trade-in value.

That was my problem. We kept ordering 10 or 20 newspapers, and I was not selling that many. But I was sure I was doing the accounting correctly. After all, the ad said I got 5¢ for every copy I sold. So, when I sold one, I put a nickel in "my" pocket and 10¢ in "their" pocket. That way, I kept the profits separate from the inventory costs.

I often walked long ways or rode my bike up to a mile or more to sell Grit. On the way home, I would stop at "Jack's Market" and spend the money in "my" pocket. There's nothing wrong with that, right? I wouldn't spend anyone else's money, just mine. Well, of course, that's not the way to do it. The hard lesson I had to learn was that you have to pay for your inventory. Period. Whether you sell some of it, or all of it. You have to pay for all of it. You can't take "your share" off the top and expect the inventory to just take care of itself.

When you're self-employed, the same thing is true about a lot of expenses. You have to pay the rent, your employees, for your inventory, for the phone, for almost everything before you get paid. Later in life, I would sometimes have to pay my employees even if I didn't get paid myself. Or hold a check to myself until it was good sometime later. But you can't "take it off the top" and expect your business to always be there for you.

After a few weeks, my parents sat me down and explained the inventory situation. They sent a check for the balance I owed and told me I was done with this business. Finished. Washed up. Well, they weren't harsh about it, but that's how I felt. But it was realistic. If you don't operate your business correctly, you will be shut down, too. Perhaps it will be by the bank. Maybe it will be by your customers who won't purchase from you any more. But you will be shut down.

Chapter 4
Don't Try it if no One Else is Doing it Already

Everyone knows that you don't go into a business when there is already someone doing the same business on every corner. It's just not good business sense. But sometimes (often actually) you can come up with an idea you realize is not already being addressed. What then?

My Dad was even more of a salesman than I am. We used to say he was one of those who could sell "icicles to Eskimos." He always had good ideas for how we could make some money. These usually required a lot of physical labor, and being a bit on the lazy side, I often didn't care for his ideas. However, one Christmas season, Dad had an idea I liked.

Everybody was getting ready for the season. Trees were selling in town. Lights and decorations were flying off the shelves. So, this was the perfect time to go door-to-door selling REAL Mistletoe!

Wait a minute... We couldn't think of anyone we knew that had ever done that before. We'd never seen someone come to our door selling mistletoe. We hadn't even seen real mistletoe sold in stores. And, wasn't part of this plant poison? Could that be an issue for selling it? We could think of lots of reasons to NOT do this.

When you get a good idea, no matter what it is, one of the first things you may think is "no one is doing this." Don't let that one thing stop you. Maybe it's not a good idea to proceed. Maybe it is a good idea. Either way, your sole criteria for your decision should not be because "no one else is doing it." If we all did that, we'd never see anything new ever again!

After some careful planning, we all set out to get some mistletoe to test our new business out. Dad took us out into the country where he knew where to find some in a tree and we took some items along with us to help bring it down. We had some string and weights so we could throw a weight tied to the string up into the mistletoe and "cut" it by dragging the string back and forth across it.

We also took the .22 cal. rifle. That was SO COOL! Dad started by shooting into the stems of the bunch hoping to hit a branch and cut it off the tree. We took turns doing this for a while until we had a basket full of fresh mistletoe. Then, we went back to put the finishing touches on it.

Mother always had done decorating of one sort or another, from flower arranging to decoupage, to just about anything else. So, she had some nice red ribbon on hand. We took the mistletoe and broke it up into small, medium and large bunches, tying each bunch with red ribbon. Then, we piled them all into our "little red wagon" and a couple of us started going door-to-door offering our wares to the neighbors.

A small sprig with a red bow tied on it was sold for $1.00. The medium sized bunch sold for about $1.50, and a large one for about $3.00. We didn't sell very many, but we did sell some! And remember, at this time, $1.00 was enough money to split between a couple of us for a trip to the store. Times were good.

Honestly, I don't remember how much money we made. I know we didn't "sell out." But we did sell some and had fun while we learned about working and being in business. Yet another great lesson for us all to learn.

We could have easily scoffed at the idea and told Dad we didn't want to do it. We could have said that we didn't want to do it because we didn't know of anyone else doing it. If we had done either, we would have missed out on a lot of fun. And, we'd have missed an opportunity that we'd always remember.

Chapter 5
Do Not Advertise Your Products

Our family owned a wholesale electronics company called Powell Electronics. Dad started the company, and invited my grandfather in to work it with him because he couldn't be on the road selling and in the store at the same time. This business grew in sales volume and in profit every year from 1959 when it was started, until about 1980.

One of the things I remember about the company is that we advertised a LOT. It seems that we advertised every way you could imagine. We ran very large newspaper ads, sometimes up to two pages at a time. We printed catalogs and distributed them. We printed flyers and distributed them. We did radio advertising. We painted the side of the building with one of the largest "billboards" in town. On one occasion, we even bought a Greyhound-style bus to use as a mobile demo studio for professional video equipment.

During one selling season, Dad had some brochures printed up with special pricing on a number of consumer based items. He wanted people in our town to see them, so we began to canvas the town, putting a filer either on the mailbox or in the door of nearly every house we came to. He would drop us off at one block and let two of us take the two sides of the street then pick us up at the end of the block. I think he got a few of the neighborhood kids to help out as well.

It was on this effort that my brother and I were about to cross a busy street when a car seemed to have come from nowhere. He was a little ahead of me and to my right. The car screeched to stop and I stopped and stretched up and back to avoid being hit. But the car hit my brother. Thankfully, he was not injured too badly. I'm not sure if he even broke a bone, but he was very sore for a while. It was very scary for everyone. Kids never seem to understand how important it is to look both ways, twice, before crossing a street.

Later on, I would have my own opportunity to assist with the advertising. We had files and files of advertising "cuts" for the various brands and models of equipment we sold. Many of our manufacturers offered co-op advertising, paying part of the cost of the advertising when we submitted the bills and the proof that we advertised their products in a way they wanted us to. This allowed us to do a lot more advertising than we would have done otherwise.

While managing one of our Hi-Fi stores, I spent a lot of time pouring through those folders looking for just the right line art for the models I wanted to advertise. At that time, we actually laid the ads out on paper. We put the lines around the ads, inserted all the photos, we wrote the words for each ad and the prices for them and had them "set" in type at the newspaper. It was a far cry from the advanced publishing we all do on our computers now.

Around 1982, I took on the design of one of our new catalogs. I still have a copy of it. A lot of the print we used was created on an old Epson dot matrix printer using special commands to condense or stretch the type of the printer. It was an early form of desktop publishing that I couldn't have done without a computer. But the computer I used was a Radio Shack Model 3 with text only screen output. We really have come a long way.

But one thing that was always clear to me is still true now: When you advertise, you get more opportunity to sell to your customers. They don't always buy, but they at least hear about your product and often come in just to see what you have. That's the opportunity you need to close the deal and make the sale.

During my senior year of college, I participated in a Business Simulation course. WE made our decisions and entered them into the computer and waited for the results. At the end, the instructor asked us what the secret was (we had tied for first place). Well, we still weren't sure but we had advertised a lot. Well, it turned out, that was the answer. If we had kept on advertising, we could have passed everyone in a flash. The more you advertised, the more products you sold. It was a good lesson to learn.

Advertising is not **the** answer, but it is important. Whether you use word-of-mouth, TV, Radio, Google Ads, or direct mail, you must let your customers know you exist and that you have solutions to their problems or the products they seek.

Chapter 6
Always Trust Everyone, Especially Yourself

While in junior high school, I was given the opportunity to work after school at my Dad's business. I would get off the bus in front of the store and work from about 3:30pm until we closed around 5:00 or 5:30pm. My responsibilities included taking out some trash, doing a little sweeping, bothering some of the people actually working, and having an afternoon snack and soda. But it paid 40¢ per hour and I was excited to be working!

At about that time, my older brother had gotten started in some of his own businesses. He had a paper route that he worked very hard to make some good money. He also had a number of small, pole-mounted vending machines that held salted peanuts. He would buy the peanuts from a local company for about $3.00 per 5 lb bag and sell them through these crank machines. For 5¢ you could get a handful of peanuts. He would place these near soda machines in factories and offices.

Each week, he would "rob" the machines and fill them with peanuts. Sometime along the way, he allowed me to do the route for a percentage of the money. I liked that, and wanted to do more. I talked with Dad and we came up with the idea of putting a metal vending shelf unit next to the soda machine in our business. I could stock it with candy bars, snacks, chips and more. It had a plastic clear window so you could see inside while it was closed and we put a cash box inside for people to place their payment when they got a snack. Dad explained that this is called "the Honor System."

Of course, in order to run a business on the honor system, you have to trust everyone that comes in contact with it. That meant every employee at my Dad's business, and some customers who went by the mini-store. It also meant I had to trust myself. When you're a pudgy 13 year old, who loves candy and snacks, and come to work from school where you probably just got out of gym class, it's probably not a good idea to "trust" yourself when it comes to the honor system and snacks in the open.

I didn't eat **all** the candy, just some of it. I probably justified what I ate knowing that with all the others paying full price for theirs, I was making enough to take one each day and still make enough profit to make the payments on the candy. Each week, I would take out the cash and count it up. Then, I'd go to the wholesaler and buy more candy and snacks.

The odd thing was, each week, when I cleaned out the box, I seemed to have enough money to buy a little less than I had bought the previous week. I think some refer to this as "inventory shrinkage." I think a more accurate term for it would be "the dis-honor system." I, and others, (whom I am sure really did plan to pay me back one day) took product without paying. The business began to disappear right before my eyes.

At some point, my Dad and I decided that it was not going to work and the cute little shelf had to go. Yes, some people complained that they really liked having the snacks on hand, but when it got down to only two types of candy bars, it was pretty sad to see.

There are people you will always trust, and you should. There are people you should never trust (and you shouldn't). But something to remember is that even good people, when given the opportunity, will sometimes make the wrong decision. The important thing is to always make a point to put checks in place to keep everyone honest. That's why we have accounting systems. That's why we use computer terminals for cashiers. It's why we always require receipts. It's not personal. It's business. And it's not really that you don't trust people. It is just that you shouldn't. It's not good business.

I once worked for a man who I am pretty sure was stealing equipment from the firm and selling it directly to customers. But because he was one of the owners, no one said a word. That business closed within a few months.

Our family has had to fire people for stealing money, for selling drugs while operating our business, for taking out merchandise hidden in the trash and picking it up later, and many other reasons. But the people weren't all bad people. They just saw an opportunity and it was too easy for them to do it. Don't make that mistake. Be sure it's not easy to steal from you. It keeps people honest.

Dad once told me "Locks are for honest people." I didn't understand that for a long time. But a lock will help an honest person stay out of something or someplace they do not belong. Dishonest people will find a way around the lock, will pick it, or cut it in order to get past it. We can't stop dishonest people. But we can help honest people to stay honest by providing locks.

Chapter 7
Work Doing Something You Hate to Do

You have probably heard the phrase "Do something you love, and you'll never work another day in your life." Well, as you may imagine, doing something you DO NOT like is going to be a lot harder.

From the time we could walk, I guess, Dad found various "chores," "jobs," and "projects" for us to do, or to help him perform. A chore could be nothing more than bringing something to the table, helping carry in the groceries, or picking up our toys. Sometimes we would be paid real cash for helping out. That was really cool. Other times, it would be something harder. Mowing the yard, building a rock wall, cleaning the bottom of the boat, or some painting project.

Occasionally, we would get matched up with a job that was really not what we wanted to do. These were usually the really hard ones. The ones that required us to actually work, maybe even sweat!

I remember one such day. I must have been ten or twelve years old. It was a hot summer day and I needed some money, and Dad needed a boat trailer painted. I'm not sure, but I think there must have been a lot of whining going on at the time.

It is important, at this point, to understand that I have never "liked" painting. Nowadays, I **can** paint. And I'm not horrible at it, but I still don't "like" to paint. It's odd, and I really don't understand why, but I just hate the idea of starting to paint. Once I get started, and I realize I'm in it till it's done, I settle down and try to enjoy it. But I still don't really like it.

From my smaller stature at that time, this trailer looked really large! And so many of the parts were *round!* That makes them even harder to paint! And if that weren't enough, he wanted me to paint it with an enamel paint with silver color! I could already see that silver stuff all over my hands and face, even my clothes and shoes! Oh, no! I did NOT want to do this job.

Of course, I didn't have a choice. That's another lesson Dad taught us. Sometimes the job is hard and takes a lot of time, but whether we want to do it or not, we have to. So, I had to just start painting. I probably painted about a foot of one piece and then I decided it was too hot, and that I needed a drink.

By the time I made it to the water fountain, Dad had caught me and told me to get back out there. The paint on the brush was drying and I needed to get busy. So, back I went. I'm sure I came up with a similar excuse every 15 minutes. But Dad just kept putting me back there. And when I thought I was done, he came out to "inspect" the work. This was his way of letting us know our shortcomings in our work. He would point out places we missed, cut corners, or forgot about all together. It was constructive criticism. But it sure sounded like he was really disappointed in me at the time.

Finally, Dad would come out for the last inspection and then he would smile, tell me I did a good job, and say something like "See, that wasn't all that bad, was it?" Only, as far as I was concerned, IT WAS that bad! I still hated it. I did it, but I hated it. And I learned something new. But it did not feel like a good learning experience at the time. I still hated it.

Imagine what it would be like for me if I had to get up every day and go paint that trailer again. What if I had to go and smell that stinky silver paint, and to hate being there, and to dread each hour and every coming day, over and over. Man, that would stink worse than that paint! Just the thought of it makes me cringe and break out in hives.

That is what it is like for millions of people every day. They continue to do the same thing every day. They continue to hate what they are doing. They continue to ignore the signs, warnings and bright flashing lights that tell them to "Get Out!" Because, for whatever reason, they either think there is nothing better, or they think they are not able to find it.

Do you love what you do? I didn't ask if you liked it. I asked if you LOVE it!?! Do you jump up in the morning ready to get to work? Do you look forward to it the night before, thinking about how you will be arranging your day? Do you come home and share all the great things that happened at work today? Do you tell your friends that you are so blessed to have the job you have? No? Well then you need to look more closely at your life.

If you don't just *love* your job, there's a good possibility that you don't *really* like it. And if you don't like it, there's a good possibility that you will start to like it less in the future. And if you... well, you see where this is going. It's not hard to hate a job that you feel stuck in, or that you don't want to be doing.

This is not an attempt to convince you that you are in a doomed job that will drive you crazy in the next few years. Nor am I trying to make you dislike your work. We all have jobs to do and, if you have a good job, that is a good thing. And, even if you do something I would hate, I hope you enjoy it. And I am thankful for you!

But before you dismiss this completely, think about what you do. If you don't love it, what is the problem? Have you forgotten how much you once loved it? Did you never like it? How did you fall into this position? Because, most people don't LOOK FOR a job they don't like. Whether you've fallen into something that stunts you, or somehow changed your mind, you need to consider finding something to do that you love.

Not that I have always loved what I have done, but I did keep changing until I found something I loved. I love being an entrepreneur. I don't always like what happens, but I love being self-employed and having to answer to me! But I won't ever work doing something I HATE again.

Chapter 8
If you can, Just Work for Your Parents

There were four boys in our family, five if you count Dad. Mother was severely outnumbered and felt it most of the time. As Dad raised us to have a good work ethic, he would start at home. I've mentioned our chores and responsibilities. Even with four boys, we were spaced so that he had help at home for quite a few years. Dad got a lot of work out of us, but it was not easy for him. We could come up with one idea after another to find ways to get out of work, but he continually tried to show us how.

Dad and Papa, my grandfather, started Powell Electronics in 1959. We grew in just about every way. We got into Hi-Fi (about the time stereo got popular!), Car Stereo systems, Television, Video, School Supplies, Satellite Receivers and just about anything else electronic someone wanted. That made for a lot of open positions. Most of us boys had the "opportunity" to work just about every job in the company at one time or another. There was always something we could do if we wanted to work.

When you're a pre-teen, there is no problem working for your Dad, but when you get into High School, it begins to look like you're a girly-man or something. Sometime around 17 years of age, people begin to think that people who work for their parents don't have to work at all. I would guess in most of the cases, it's much harder than people would imagine, but the truth is seldom known by youth.

With that many opportunities in a growing business, Dad *could have* made room for us from the time we started driving until the business closed. But Dad had been working with his father for several years now and he understood that what we really needed was an opportunity to work for *someone else.*

We were given opportunities on several occasions to work for others. There was even a day or two that we were taken to my uncle's farm to haul hay. But most of us were given opportunities to work for my dad's friends or business associates. He would find out who needed someone, and then "volunteer" us to take the job.

There were two such jobs I remember during high school. One job was at a sewing factory, and the other in a butcher shop at a local grocery store. One was more "educational" in format, the other more "physical" in nature. I learned important lessons in both jobs, and I've always been glad to have had the opportunities.

After my junior year of high school, Dad asked a friend if he had a place for me that summer. There was another young man about my age whose father also asked the same man for a job for the summer. So, he took both of us in to work in the plant. But this man, Aaron Yarvin, was a very smart man. Strict and calculating, he ran his plant well and taught us more than a few things about the world.

In order to justify having us on hand, he "created" a job for us. But it would be one that would benefit the company in the long run. Each of us was to take a department and "observe" what goes on there. Ask questions, get information, and write up a set of "Standard Operating Procedures" for each department. Mark, my counter part, worked from the receiving department toward the factory, and I started in the shipping department, working backward toward the factory. We would then meet somewhere in the middle by summer's end.

When we thought we had our "report" ready, Mr. Yarvin would have us read them to him. Then he would tear it apart, asking questions, showing us where we needed more detail, asking why we said one thing or another. It was like going to the principal every other day. But we really honed our skills.

Between Mr. Yarvin and a great High School Senior English teacher, I was able to test my way through both English Composition and ½ of English Literature in college!

Mr. Yarvin taught me several very important lessons: from "when to keep your mouth shut" to "when to mind your own business." I learned a lot more than some silly details about how a plant worked. In fact, he even made me PAINT for a few days! But it was very good to know what it was like to work for someone else.

That is a lesson you really need if you work for family. I know from experience that your family *can* teach you what you need to know. But working for someone else lets you see the other side of things. To know what it FEELS like to be on the "employee" side of things. To be taught some different lessons than those of your family. It is almost a *necessity* to round out your understanding of work in general.

After I got my degree, I considered working somewhere else. I even considered working several states away from my family's business. But in the end, came back to work at home. I learned a lot more by doing that. I was able to work in every department, do almost every job, learn how to hone my selling skills, and get great life lessons. Eventually, I spun off a business from that one while the original business faltered. I continued successfully in that spin-off for five additional years before selling it.

It's ok to work for your parents or other family, but don't *just* work for them.

Chapter 9
Believe Everything You Are Told

    The other of the two jobs outside the family business was the butcher shop. I had no idea what job I had, Dad just said he called someone and I would be working for him. I was told to report to Liberty Super Market on Friday afternoon and I would be set up for the job. I already knew my "boss," we had attended the same church for years. So, I knew I would recognize him and knew his children. So, I went in looking for him.

    The first day was a blur. I filled out some paper work, was shown where everything was, and was told I'd be doing "clean up" in the shop. There was a young man, about four or five years my elder, who had worked there for years. He started where I was and was about to become a full-time butcher. So, he was to show me the ropes and teach me how to do each job.

    I had fun the first couple of days. But by the third or fourth day, I was starting to feel pretty overwhelmed. They told me I was responsible to clean everything by myself. There was just no way I would be able to get everything done that I was being shown. I was sure that I was doomed to failure. What had Dad gotten me into? In my previous book "*Wizbits from Dad*" I have a "wizbit" about this very day. I went to Dad after work, extremely upset, and told him I could not do the job. He talked me down, told me a story about his early work experience, and gave me the secret: **If you can't get it done today, it will be there tomorrow. And if it's important that it get done today, someone will pitch in to help you get it done.**

    Armed with that reassurance, I came in the next day with a song in my heart and dancing to the beat! The other shop workers could hardly believe the change overnight. But I think I did have a little Bi-Polar thing going most of my life. From that day forward, I did what I could. I did a good job at it, and when it was important, someone helped me. We got the job done and I hated to leave when it came time to go to college that fall.

Many businesses are like this, too. When you get started, suddenly people come out of the woodwork telling you what you will have to do, how you will have to do it, and that there is no way you will be successful at this. Even statistics themselves scream that over 50% of new business will fail before they are four years old. But you don't have to believe them.

Not everything people will tell you is true or will come true. This is the case with both good and bad things. Things probably won't be as bad as they say it will be, but then again, they may. And it probably won't be all upward and onward like you would like to believe, but then again, maybe it will. But if you start off your business, or change in the middle, thinking that what *they* tell you is true, then you will not get the enjoyment you could be getting from your business.

Part of the "soul" of a business is in the mind of the creator of that business. The possibilities, the ways they can help others, the success they will see down the road… all that is part of your belief system. Don't give it up for promises or prophecies. If we all believed just what we were told, we'd all fail.

Chapter 10
Give Up Before You Have A Chance To Make It Work

The first time I actually tried to start a business that was just my own, it was a small mail-order business. It was about 1981 and I had finally given in to having my first "home computer." It was a $479 Ohio Scientific C1P Series II computer with a 6502 microprocessor, 4K of RAM, and 8K BASIC in ROM. To load a program, you used a cassette recorder to play the tape into the computer input. To save, you "printed" it out through the sound port to the cassette recorder.

It was a fascinating time and from the moment I got my computer, I spent way too much time on it. But I learned something every day. There were a few of us who got them at the same time and began a "club" of sorts. Sharing information, programs, and ideas. I found out what kind of memory chips my computer used and found a place to order some. They came in, I placed them in my computer, and they worked! WOW! That was easy!

I found that many other users of this brand, and similar brands, used the same chips. But they didn't really know how to buy parts like someone who had grown up in an electronics company, so I started ordering them for friends. There was a magazine specifically for 6502 based computers called *Micro 6502*. I put together a small ad and a few months later, it came out. I advertised a "Free Catalog." Just send $1 and an SASE (Self-Addressed-Stamped-Envelope) and I would mail the catalog back to you.

The catalog was hand typed on a portable Smith-Corona typewriter. I had chips, chip sets, some software I had written and some other odds and ends in the catalog. It was the coolest thing going to the mailbox and getting envelopes with one-dollar bills in them. I copied the pages of the catalog on blue paper in my dad's office, stapled them together, and mailed them for about 13¢ or so. I made money on every catalog I mailed.

The orders were not far behind. I have no idea how much I sold, but I do remember shipping a number of cassettes and ordering up to 100 or more memory chips at a time more than a few times. So, I must have sold a few hundred dollars' worth. I still have one of the first envelopes I received with the same dollar bill in a frame next to my desk as I type now. The letter in it was dated June 6th, 1981.

The company was called Software Plus. I suggested that we sold software PLUS a lot more. I wrote two or three small programs, listed more chips and hoped to build this into something big. I had a chance. I had as much a chance as any other company. Up until then, electronic parts companies advertised to electricians and hobbyists. Now, there was a new marketplace: Computer Enthusiasts. I was one of the first to recognize that. It was a real opportunity.

In 1981, we had a one-year-old son. We also had a car payment, a house payment, a utility and cable payment, and probably a furniture payment. Since I was working for Dad at this time, either he or I probably decided that I needed to concentrate on what I was doing for a living, not waste time on a dream of some kind.

So, after I completed all my obligations, I let Software Plus go the way of several more to follow. I set it aside and worked at my "real" job to make a living. Could it have become big? Maybe; maybe not. I'll never know. But I'll always feel like I let it go and gave up before I even gave it a chance to be a success. I'm still proud of the dollar on the wall. It reminds me that if you have an idea, any idea, you can still try to make it work. You don't have to be rich. You don't have to be a genius. You don't even have to be really smart (although that does help…). But you have to try, and you have to give it a chance. Or… you'll never know.

Chapter 11
Listen to that ONE Naysayer

Most entrepreneurs have ideas. They have lots of ideas. The ideas just keep on coming, and coming and coming some more. There seems to be no shortage of them. But, of course, not all the ideas are good. Some are good and should be tried. Some are horrible and should never be attempted.

Here's a freebie for you: Find someone who will listen and think before they shoot you down. You need someone like that to tell your ideas to. Otherwise, you'll start thinking all your ideas are bad and stop telling people about them.

When you tell people your ideas, you will get their opinions in return. Opinions are like so many other things. I'll use elbows as an example. Everybody has them, and most of them are not worth much. You probably have a similar example that may or may not be more tasteful.

These opinions you are given are gold. Pure gold. But it's not always easy to find. You have to really dig to find the gold in them. Some of the opinions are multipliers for your idea. Some of them are absolute viruses for them and kill the ideas in an instant. But you *have* to ask for them. It's the only way to find out if you're on to a good one or not.

Often, you'll find that several people will like an idea, and several will not like it. This could be for any of a number of reasons. The simplest is that people are different. They don't see things the same, they don't understand things equally, and they have different views of just about everything. So, you should always expect to have a number of people on either side of a new idea.

When you find an idea that *everyone* likes, you should really consider that idea as one that has merit. If everyone really thinks it is a great idea, then the likelihood that you will be successful is way up there. Not guaranteed, of course, but way up there.

When you present an idea and *nobody* likes it. RUN AWAY!!! That's a bad idea. Of course, once in a blue moon, you'll come across an idea that is good no matter how many people don't like it. But don't think for a minute that ALL your ideas are like that. They're not.

Once, I had an idea that I spent a long time considering. I did my research. I asked a lot of people. I talked to people in similar businesses. I looked for a good location for the business. I did just about everything but kick it off.

The idea was for a used record store. The time was about 1985 and vinyl records had been given a "death knell" by the Cassette and oncoming Compact CD. I had visited a store in Nashville, TN that was about the size of a football field inside. They had vinyl records of all kinds, comic books, baseball and football cards, and just about every other kind of collectible you could imagine.

I had grown up with vinyl. I had about 200 LPs (long playing records, or albums). They covered the gambit from hard rock, to gospel, to classical, to comedy and even folk music. I knew that even at used record prices, I could start with my own collection and have a decent place to start. And I had talked with the owner of the store in Nashville about obtaining a starting inventory.

The record store owner explained to me that he had lots of duplicates and could pull a little of everything to give me a wide range of records and artists in all kinds of price ranges. I could buy $1,000 worth of records and get enough to stock about half my store to open. The records would sell for as little as 50¢ or $1 and up to $5-$10 each.

How do you make money, you ask? That's the fun part. People bring in their used records to sell. Each record is examined to put it in a category to be priced. Considerations included its relative popularity, how high it went on the charts, the artist, the condition of the jacket, and the condition of the record itself. (Scratches on records would make pops and clicks on a record player or turntable). The higher it ranked, the more you could pay for it.

Prices paid were done in stacks. "This stack, I'll pay $2 each. The next stack, I'll pay $3 each. All the rest, I don't want, but I'll give you 10¢ each, or 25¢ each." Usually, the customer had already decided they didn't want to keep the records and would take whatever you offered. If not, they were free to take what they liked and keep the others. But you never pay more than half the amount for which a record will sell.

So, I had the concept down and I was pretty sure it would work. What about a location? Good question! In business, as in all real estate, the secret is Location! Location! Location! Well, I had a great location in mind. The local University of North Alabama was located at the north end of Court Street in Florence, AL where I lived. It was about two blocks from the business district. Students would often walk from school to downtown.

I found a small store with a bay window located on the first cross street south of the university. It was behind the town's best bakery and across the main street from a large "five and dime" department store. It was the perfect place to put a record store that would be close to the most likely customers, college students. And, of course, I could hire college students to run the place when I couldn't be there.

The name I had chosen was *perfect* too! I planned to call it "The Used Record Store." That way, when someone asked: "Where are you going?" the answer would be "to the used record store." The very name described exactly what it was! This could not lose!

I asked all my friends. They all loved the idea. I asked my wife. Even SHE liked the idea, but she will always support anything I do. She always has. I asked my brothers, they thought it was a good idea. Everyone I asked about it liked the idea and encouraged me to do it. Everyone except for one, that is. My dad did not think it would work.

We spent a long time talking about it. But remember, I worked for Dad. Anything I did would surely take me away from my work, reduce my participation in the business, and cause me to be less efficient. He also felt that it would be a good way for me to lose my money. He could see me wasting a lot of time and getting nothing in return. He, too, had experienced failure in business and he didn't want me to do the same.

After a lot of consideration, I decided that Dad's opinion trumped all the others and I took his advice. I let the idea go and moved on. But occasionally, I would look back.

The University of North Alabama has continued to grow over the years. It has expanded in all directions. Downtown Florence has since gone through a down time and is back on the rise again. Another record store in town at the time soon began to carry used records. They bought, sold, and traded vinyl from that time until now. They're still in business and from what I understand, do quite a good business.

That could have been me. I can feel it in my bones. But, I decided to listen to the ONE naysayer who said I couldn't. I chose to not go that direction. Would I have been a success? Maybe. I'll never know. But I didn't do it, so, I have yet another one of those "what if's" hanging in my past. I'm sure that God knew where I'd need to be and chose to help me toward that location. But I'll always wonder if it would have been that kind of job that you absolutely love to go to every day.

Listen to your friends. Listen to your family. Listen to the promoters. Listen to the naysayers. But don't let them make your decision for you. Make the decision. Move on. And never look back.

Chapter 12
Don't do the Math

When Compact Discs came out in the late 1980's, everyone who was into stereo equipment or music knew they were **The Next Big Thing.** At that time, I ran a computer store, which was already one of the next big things. We were selling Apple and Macintosh computers, and doing pretty well with them. But the man who was my store manager, and one of the salesmen and I thought that there must be a gold mine in selling CDs. After all, anyone who was anyone would soon have a CD player, they sounded much better than cassette tapes, and they were DIGITAL!!

So, the three of us decided what we really needed was a side business that would take up all our spare time and all our spare money and flush it down the toilet. Wait, that's not right! We needed a successful CD store that sold nothing but the latest CDs for all to buy! After all, you could only buy them in about 12 places around town already!

Of course, I'm already letting the cat out of the bag, so let me back up and tell the story.

The three of us each put in $5000 to get started. We were so sure this would be a success that we just knew it was the right thing to do. The store I currently rented had a small section that we had been using as a classroom for computing in the evenings that we decided would be large enough to turn it into a store for us. That would save us some rent until we could get on our feet.

Because it was in the same building, we could take turns checking on things "next door" to make sure everything was going well. We could hire some part-time students to man the store for us and we could work it in the evenings, taking turns again, to share the savings of not paying an employee.

We spent about $10,000 on buying CDs from a distributor. Going through that list and trying to decide what everyone else would want to buy was a real chore, but it was also very exciting! But $10,000 didn't go very far. CDs sold at retail for $14-$20 or so and since we were buying from a distributor, we had to pay $8-16 for them. There wasn't a big margin in them because we were only buying in small quantities, usually only one of each CD.

Next, we spent money putting in paneling, although a lot was already there. We still had to paint, arrange, build boxes for showcasing the CDs, and get the store ready for our first customers. We opened a few of the CDs to listen to while we were working. (Oh yeah, we had to install a stereo system to play CDs while customers were in there.) We brought in the few we had purchased and played them to keep the music going while we worked. It's amazing how quickly you can get tired of CDs playing when you only have about 5-10 to listen to.

Finally, the day came for us to open and we started "pushing" people from the computer store next door to shop. But most of them were more interested in the latest computer game than in music, so not many purchased. But we knew it was just a matter of time. So, we figured we would do some promotion.

We printed up some "coupons" for $2 off each CD purchased and started passing them around to all our friends and even to strangers as we went, hoping they'd buy one and then keep coming back. But night after night, we sat there with very little business, listening to the same old 5-10 CDs and wondering why no one was coming into the store.

Since this store was in an area that was mostly open just in the daytime, we decided that we needed to get to a better shopping area. One where a lot of people would come buy on a regular basis. We soon found a store front near the local Wal-Mart. This Wal-Mart was the busiest Wal-Mart in all of the Southeast for some reason, so this HAD to be a good place to be.

(Never mind that Wal-Mart also sold CDs, and, at a discount.) The location we found was formerly a Cinnabon™ store, that had closed for some reason that we could not figure out. (I don't know, maybe LACK OF SALES?) It even still smelled like cinnamon buns!

We paid more to have a big sign made, paid more for the space, and even had to pay a percentage of our sales to the landlord. But we were now going to be SET to make it big! We continued selling computers by day and CDs by night. Each night all three of us would stop by at some time to see how it was going. Some days, we would sell 3 or 4 CDs, and other days, as many as 5-6. Sometimes, we may even sell 10 CDs!! What a racket!

We just didn't get it. Why were sales so low? What was the problem? Why were we not being inundated with customers looking for more of the **next big thing?**

At some point, we decided we needed a larger inventory and that we should all three put an additional $5000 each into it. The other two did, but when I went to the bank, my banker, whom I consider to have been a real friend at the time, told me "no." I was too far stretched out to borrow more money. So, I was not able to put in my part. That hurt me at the time. But it was the right decision for the bank. And it was the right decision for me.

We continued until we had been working like this for over a year. Still very few sales, no profits and we were bleeding money every month. I finally told the other two that we should shut it down. They disagreed and I finally "sold" them my stock for basically nothing and walked away from my investment. Since I had bought stock and sold it, I was able to take a loss on my taxes and recoup a little of it in deductions.

The other two men continued to run it for another year or so, finally having to give up and they both ended up with a hundred CDs or so each for their $10,000 investment. It was not pretty.

So, why did this happen? What was wrong? Were CDs the next big thing? YES! So, what was wrong? In simple terms: **We didn't do the math.**

Looking back, I was able to analyze the situation. There was nothing wrong with our idea, or plans, but had we done the math, we'd have waited a while to do it.

CDs were new. In fact, CD Players were new. Not many people owned a CD Player. I did, but my family owned a Stereo Business. The other two partners did, but they were techy people that loved new toys and good music. But most people were still buying vinyl (the first time around) and Cassettes for their music. So, I tried to do some math...

In the two county area that we lived in, there were probably about 120,000 people. Figuring about 4 people per home, that's 30,000 homes. Since they were new, I figured that maybe if you were optimistic that up to 10% might have a CD Player. That puts us at 3,000 players.

Now, not everyone buys a CD or even an album every week, so if we figured that each week, maybe 10% bought a new CD, that would mean 300 CDs bought each week. Now, we weren't the only store in town. There was another record store that sold them, two WalMarts, a K-Mart or two, perhaps even a few other stores, so maybe 10 or more stores sold them. And we were the smallest of all of them.

If we had gotten "our fair share" of 1/10 of the sales of all CDs purchased within a week for the two-county area, we would have sold 30 CDs each week. Well, we were selling 3-10 per day, so we were actually doing pretty well considering the choices. But at a profit of $4-5 each, even 50 CDs per week would only bring in less than $250/week in profit. That wouldn't cover the cost of the rent, much less the cost of employees, insurance, taxes, etc.

Had we "done the math" up front, we'd have never opened that store. Or, we'd have watched the market and waited for the time when people couldn't find enough CDs to buy, and THEN opened it. But, we wouldn't have thrown over $25,000 into a black hole either.

Whatever you're planning, whatever the product is, whatever you THINK it can do, **DO THE MATH FIRST**. It will save you a lot of trouble, heartache, time away from your family, and money. Always do the math first.

Chapter 13
Over Diversify Your Business

Our family business was an electronics company. At least, it started out that way. Dad began by selling antennas for TVs, electrical tape, a few tubes, and the like. But he soon found out that he could buy almost anything wholesale once he was in business. Customers asked if he sold antenna towers, so he found a company to buy from and started buying and selling them. Then, it was parts for radios and TVs. Resistors, capacitors, tubes, picture tubes, knobs, kits, and more.

In the 1960's, schools began to put TVs in all the classrooms. They knew they'd need them because by the end of the decade, President Kennedy had promised that we'd put a man on the moon and bring him back safely. So, we started selling Televisions. And we sold a lot of them. And not just to schools, we got the dealership for Sony™ for our area and ended up with a large TV showroom.

Then, Video came out. First, we got into the big professional video. At this time, a video recorder was about the size of two of the largest suitcases you've ever seen and weighed so much it took at least two grown men to move one around. The tape was on large 2" thick reels and it was just black and white! But we sold them. We sold Ampex, then Sony, then Panasonic, RCA, JVC and others. We sold just about every kind of video thing you could imagine.

Since we were selling to schools, we began to sell language labs, and TV studios, and then Audio-Visual equipment like overhead projectors, opaque projectors, slide projectors, 16mm film projectors, and of course, they all needed screens, so we sold wall and ceiling mounted screens of all sizes. We sold curtains to schools, and even stage curtains, along with ordering gym and playground equipment for them and much more. It seemed that we couldn't go wrong. The more we offered, the more we sold. So, we got into selling school supplies.

My mother headed up this division and it did very well! We sold everything you needed for schools. Bulletin board aids, workbooks, pens, pencils, erasers, toys, pads, notebooks... you name it, we sold it. And we sold a lot of it. We had a glossy catalog that was over 1/2" thick packed with all the stuff you could buy for schools. This included complete intercom systems, fire alarms, sound systems for auditoriums, gyms, and ball fields. You could hardly name something that we didn't sell or couldn't buy to sell to you.

Later, we got into High Fidelity Stereo sales and opened a complete new division for it. We had two stores in Birmingham, AL, one in Florence and one in Sheffield at one time. One of the largest stereo companies in the state if not the Southeast! We were big distributors or dealers for many of the big names including JBL, Pioneer, Advent and many more. We sold car stereo too! We became a master distributor for Craig car stereo and home electronics. We were huge!

When I went to college in the mid 1970's and came back with computer experience, I was convinced that we needed to sell computers. Eventually, we got into selling them and of course, we sold them to the schools in droves! Then, we got the Apple dealership due to the local reps not being very pro Apple and to me writing a letter to Apple telling them why they needed us!

From 1959, until about 1980, the company sold more and made more profit every year. It seemed that we couldn't grow fast enough, or sell enough things to meet all the demand. It was the time of dreams.

In the early 1980's, a former employee came to my dad and told him "he needed" to bid on some very large projects being done nearby. He said he could almost guarantee him the business. That there would be lots of profit, and all he had to do was just underbid the lowest bidder, and this guy had an inside and could find out how much the low bid was. It sounded really sweet! This was a huge bid on two extremely large "profitable" contracts. How could we lose? So, we placed a bid.

The next few years were the hardest I think my Dad ever had to endure. One after another, things became clear that caused problem after problem. First, the company that we underbid had not considered all the items in the bid. They left a LOT out. A WHOLE Lot. But, we had to supply it because we were the winning bid.

Next, Dad had to just about walk away from his successful business to take care of all the issues that were coming up in these big contracts. He spent a lot of time on the job sites, working with subcontractors, figuring out how to come up with all the items that he was told were included that he knew nothing about. It was a nightmare; for all of us.

In the long run, it was the straw that broke the camel's back. It took so much out of Dad, so much out of the business, and so much out of the employees, that it virtually killed the successful business he had built. In 1986, I spun the computer business out on it's own, and Dad let the other business close.

There were other contributing factors, of course. The state had a few years earlier enacted "Proration" where they unilaterally cut funding to all schools by 10% for a few years. This eliminated much of the "extras" that schools could buy, and a lot of what we were selling. During this time, we sold off the School Supply business. That company ran for several years and eventually closed as well. And the big "box" stores began to carry almost everything we sold. For many years, if you wanted any kind of electronics, you came to our store. That was no more.

I believe we could have survived almost all of these things had it not been for the fact that we sold so many different kinds of things, that we couldn't do justice to any of the particular areas anymore. We had over diversified the business to death.

Later, in a consulting company I own, I nearly did the same thing. Having been very acquainted with the Apple and Macintosh lines, I had built a consulting business on those computers and had done well. I added employees and started doing work on PCs as well as Macs. The problem was, I didn't have the skills to do that work and found myself billing customers for time spent learning how to fix the problems they were paying us to remedy. When I realized I had "over diversified", I put a stop to it. I didn't want to make the same mistake. I sold that part of my business to a company in town that is still successful. I apologized to my PC customers, even giving refunds to some of them. And I shrank my business down by laying people off.

That was hard to do. But I had seen what could happen. I was not going to make the same mistake. As a result, I'm still self-employed. All my former employees are doing very well, and I've saved my business for another day.

Chapter 14
Be Under-Capitalized

When things started getting tough in our family business, I began to notice that it was getting harder and harder to work through inventory issues. Customers began to pay later, we began offering longer terms, we would be on "credit hold" with one company until we sold enough of another company's inventory to pay the first, and then we'd get an order from the first company. Of course, then, we'd be on "credit hold" with the second company and have to sell some of a third company's inventory to pay them, and so on and so on. We just couldn't catch up.

There were a few reasons for this dilemma. First, we were selling at lower margins. When you don't have much profit, you can't catch up. Second, the large contracts and slowdowns mentioned earlier were "robbing" us of needed cash. And third, we were trying to move too fast for the amount of cash flow we had available. In short, we were undercapitalized.

It's easy to get into this situation. We had two signs up that we tried to remind ourselves of when we were making "deals." The first one read: **"We'll just lose $1 on each product and make it up in volume."** The second read: **"One more good deal and we'll be out of business!"** Both signs reminded us that you can't make money giving away product. You must make a good profit on it to stay in business.

When you start a new business, there's a HUGE temptation to "buy" business to get going. You know, undercut whoever is selling out there now, so that customers will come to you to buy. But that never works in the long run. One of two things will happen. 1) You'll eventually have to go back up and that customer you "gained" will be lost to whomever is offering the lowest price. Or 2) You won't be able to stay in business to serve them because you can't make enough profit.

There are things you CAN do to get business, and they're not all that hard. But few are willing to work for the business the way you must. These things include being honest ALWAYS. Being up front with customers. Doing what is best for the customer. Letting the customer know HOW you're taking care of them. Reminding customers that you will be there to support them. All these help bring in customers. But cutting prices is not a long-term solution.

The problem with under-capitalization is that it is an on-going issue that continues to crop up every time you need to do something. If you don't have the cash flow or the money, you can't do anything. You can't spruce up the office or store front when needed. You can't do something special for the employees who are so dedicated. You can't take any money out of the business for your own use. You can't take on new lines or additional inventory. In short, it freezes you in your tracks.

In every business in which I have been either an owner, or part owner, during my lifetime to date, we have been under-capitalized. And... it stinks. You can make it in a business without enough capital, but it is REALLY HARD. Not impossible, but you really have to be able to roll with the punches. You have to be ready to dodge things thrown at you from the right and the left. And get really creative with how you handle your money. Did I mention it was hard?

When I "spun off" the computer store from the family business, Dad was still my partner. We ran it the best we could and took advantage of the "head-start" we'd gotten while being under the umbrella of the larger business. We started out with inventory and sales and some assets. But we had to keep selling to make it work. And we did. And our profits were very good too! We sold computer systems at an average of 40% margin for a few years after that before margins started to fall. And we kept 4-5 people employed as we grew the business.

In 1986, the year we started that company, we probably did around $250,000-$300,000 in sales. Maybe more than that. And at a good profitable rate. But there were four employees that year, so we needed more sales to keep payroll going. We continued to grow, order more, and sell more every year. But, we didn't have the capital to fund the growth. We used the only option open to us: Floor Planning.

Here's how floor planning worked... you could buy almost anything you wanted from the company (in this case Apple, Inc.) and "charge" it through the finance company. They would take inventory each month to verify that you were paying for product as you sold it. If they inventoried and found things missing, you wrote them a check for those items right there on the spot. And for everything else, you paid interest at the current rates plus a few percentage points. And at that time, (look it up if you don't believe me) we were paying in excess of 20% interest on a lot of what we kept in stock.

It allowed us to stay in business, but ate away at our profits. Little by little, it began to get harder to pay bills, keep caught up on inventory, and make sales when we needed to. By the late 1980's, we were set to do about $900,000+ for the year and things were tight, but moving forward.

About that time, I received a request for a bid from a local school board for some PC computers. We had begun to sell some by then and we were familiar with them and even did service on them, so I placed a bid. I called our distributor and got pricing, told them it was for a bid and then used those prices to mark them up and place the bid for about 20-25 computer systems. It would be a good order if we won the bid.

The bids were opened and we got the business! I was excited. I called the distributor to check my order and when I asked to confirm the prices, they said I must be crazy! They couldn't sell them to me at those prices, they were cost prices. I proclaimed that their salesman had given me those prices, but I had no written quote so they wouldn't honor them. Well, I still had to fulfill the bid, so I asked about pricing and started working on filling the order at little or no profit.

Then, they told me they could not sell them to me on credit. They had put me on credit hold because of a very old invoice that was still outstanding. They had not sent me a bill for the invoice, nor told me that I was on credit hold, nor that I had anything due to them. But I had bought $1,000's of dollars of equipment and software from them in the mean time with Collect On Delivery. They didn't care. I was not getting credit from them no matter what. So, I called our bank.

Our family business had closed and had paid the bank every cent they owed them and had worked out deals with all the other creditors, returning product, settling some debts, etc. But, in the bank's eyes, we had gone bankrupt. We had not. We never filed for bankruptcy, and took care of the bank in full, but they were not going to loan me any money.

Finally, I accepted defeat, called the School Board, and told them I could not honor my bid. It was one of the saddest days in my business history. I literally went to my office, closed the door, and had a little pity party during which, I believe I shed a few tears. I hated to disappoint a customer. It really pained me to have come to this.

The problem was... I didn't have enough capital to fund the business I was trying to run. I should have cut back somewhere, sold out some part of what was gathering dust, laid off some employees or something to fix it, but I was still learning and didn't know what to do. We ended up selling out to a competitor in the next town. For a year or so, I worked for him while he ended up running both our businesses into the ground.

More lessons learned. Be very careful what you try to do with the money you have. Not having enough for your plans and circumstances has killed many a business. But once you've been there, you really don't want to go back. You'll learn quickly. But it would be better if you just took my advice. Don't be undercapitalized. It's not fun.

Chapter 15
Believe that "if they can do it, I can do it!"

If you have an entrepreneur spirit at all, then at some point, someone will recognize it and call you up and say something like: "Hey, I've got a business opportunity I'd like to discuss with you and see what you think." Once in a while, it turns out to be a legitimate business opportunity, but most of the time, they mean Multi-Level Marketing, or MLM.

They will tell you about people *they know* who are making six-figure incomes from just telling their friends about the products. And guess what? You don't have to do much of anything! The people under you do all the work! *It's easy! Anyone can do it!*

I will **NOT** tell you that all MLMs are bad. Nor will I tell you that you can't be successful in managing a MLM business. Because you may be suited to just that kind of business. In fact, my father was VERY Successful in a MLM business. He made it "big" with a 5-6 figure salary, the "free" car, and numerous awards and trips. He was highly suited to that business. And he sincerely believed in the products.

But what I will do is caution you about MLM businesses. As was just indicated, they are not for everybody. Some thrive in them and some fail miserably. Most try it for a while, have a modicum of success, then let it go. You can waste a lot of time and money in an MLM and perhaps I can help you avoid that kind of business *if it is not for you.*

I, too, got started in an MLM business early on in my marriage. The two of us had a new baby and wanted to make some extra income. We had friends in the business and a distributor/manager who told us about all the income she was making and the trips she took, etc. It sounded fantastic. And the products were good. Vitamins, soaps, cleansers, and more. We used them and encouraged our family and friends to use them as well.

We got copies of cassette tapes of all the big sellers in the company who shared their secrets about selling along with doctors who really believed and trusted in the products and recommended and sold them to their patients. We heard stories about everything from success to downright miracles as a result of the program and the products. It was invigorating!

Most MLMs operate the same way. First, you sign up. This is a fairly easy process. Just fill in a form, pay a modest amount, usually $25-$50, and "Presto!" you're in! You can now purchase products at wholesale prices and begin to earn points. Points are not dollars, they're points. The more points you earn, the bigger the discounts you receive and the bigger your bonuses are. Each company is different and they call their points by different names, but basically, you get more points for selling the more profitable items.

Once you've been "set up," then the next step is to believe in your products. So, you should buy the products for your own use. Of course, the products will save you money over what you've been buying, so it's not a hard sell to yourself, just buy them and start saving money. So, you spend $300-$500 getting a little bit of everything you should be using and taking (vitamins, etc.) and start believing in the products.

The third step is to then introduce the products and the product line to your friends and family. The general thought is that if everyone you knew would just buy and use the products, you'd be a success and earn a lot of extra income. So, you try to convince everyone you know to do the same things you are doing.

Of course, the best way to do this is by going to "meetings." A meeting usually has someone speak who gets everyone pumped up and ready to go to make big bucks. After that, they talk about how to sell and convince people to try the products, etc. The more meetings you go to, the more you'll believe and the more you can sell. And the more people you can get to go to the meetings with you, the more they'll buy.

Somewhere along the line, you start to realize a few things. First, you realize that you have very little home life left. Most nights are spent talking with people about the business, or going to meetings, or calling people on the phone to arrange for a meeting. This can be good, or this can be bad. If you are a person with very little in your life, this can be an absolute God-Send for you. Having a reason to be with people, mingle, share, talk, etc., can be a real boost for a lot of people. If you thrive on this kind of activity, then you may love it. Most of us, however, especially at the age they try to get you started, have families, small children, bills to pay, and jobs to do. It's not easy to give up your home life to make a few extra dollars per month.

The next thing you notice is that you're building up an inventory. Again, this can be a good thing if you're turning that inventory on a regular basis. But often, the inventory sits there as you wait for someone to think they may need the exact product you bought to have on hand. Eventually, when you stop trying to sell, you're stuck with a lot of inventory that you neither need nor want. And you paid for all of that inventory. Sometimes hundreds of dollars. And it is just sitting there.

Finally, you'll realize that people are dodging you in public. They don't want to talk with you because you always want to convince them to be "in your business." They are not interested, don't want to do it, and can't see the opportunity. But, you've been told that "anyone who produces fog on a mirror when they have one put up to their nose is a prospect and must be sold!" So, you end up alienating all your friends and family.

I'll say it again; this is just ONE of the ways it can turn out. People who love this kind of business run ads for people to call in to learn more. They pass out literature that just offers a business opportunity and don't push. They are professional about how they go about it. They thrive on the opportunity to find the next person who wants to make it big (under them, of course) and train them to do just that. If you are that kind of person, I applaud you and encourage you to continue. If this doesn't sound like your kind of thing, you'd probably be better off to look for something else.

MLMs are some of the most successful companies in the world. They are because people buy-in, believe in their products and the program, and they work the program and use the products. But they're just not for everyone.

Another time, a friend had me convinced that I should get into another MLM. I was ready to sign up and pay the $35. After all, he said they would help me get my down-line and it would be very little work for me. It would be easy! I'd be making money in no time! I told my wife I was about to sign up. She said, "I don't want you to do it." And I replied "that's ok, I'll do all the work, you won't have to do anything." And she repeated it. So, I replied, "We don't have to have meetings here, so you don't have to worry about people coming into our home." She then said: "I don't think you are listening. I don't want you to do it. I don't want you to alienate our friends and family. I don't want people to avoid us because you'll always be selling to them. **I** don't want **YOU** to do it."

Finally, I heard her. And I understood. And she was right. And I turned the offer down. I am not one who thrives in MLM. We had already had too many of my "side gigs" take up too much of our home time. I didn't need to do this. So, I didn't. And I have not regretted it.

Not all the MLMs are the same, and there's an MLM for almost any kind of product. Jewelry, storage containers, baskets, vitamins, cleaners, air and water purifiers, you name it. If you're sincerely interested in working one of those businesses, and just LOVE the product you'll be selling, and are prepared to work and extreme amount of time, then DO IT! You may love it!

But just remember, just because someone else is making the big six-figure income doing it, doesn't mean you will. Only those that work an MLM FULL-TIME PLUS are that successful.

It must become your life, not just a vocation. So, don't go into one unless you plan to make it your life as well.

Chapter 16
Don't Try New Things

By now you have realized that I have ~~failed~~ (no that's not right) not been fully successful in a lot of businesses. Sure, I've had my share of disappointments and business ideas that didn't pan out, but I still kept on trying new things. This appears to be one of the marks of the serial entrepreneur: they have a new idea everyday of how someone could make money.

I have a close friend who calls me at least once a week with his next "Million Dollar Idea." Each has its own merits and some are downright great ideas. He doesn't have the time to pursue them all, and neither do I. But occasionally, I'll listen and get some good ideas just from his ideas.

As I have indicated, I have always worked toward the goal of being productive and finding a way to earn money. I have one of those little notebooks where you store all your contacts' business cards so you can reference them when needed. Only, mine is full of MY business cards. For years (at least since I've had access to a laser printer), I've made business cards for most of my businesses. So, I have plenty. I don't have one for everything I've tried, but I do have a lot of them.

I just counted over 35 business cards in that little folder. These represent my positions in about 10-15 companies and/or businesses I've started or worked for. Some of them were big companies like Apple Computer and BOEING along with our family business I worked in for about 8 years. But a LOT of them are for startups that I thought could be big. A few made it for a while, and some fizzled out before they ever got started.

But one thing I know: These new ideas and new business tactics have kept me alive, fed me and my family, and helped me learn one thing after another until I've built up a wealth of information about business and how to operate one. I have become the proverbial "Jack of all trades, and Master of none." But, the things I've learned along the way make me more prepared than ever to help out in a business, or run one of my own.

There have been times when things were really tough for us. Especially the times when I had to go from making a lot of money to making about half what I was making just prior to that. And there have been good times when I had several employees and lots of clients and brought in lots of income. But for some reason, it has been difficult for me to stick with just one thing and work it all the way through. I struggle with that. But looking back, I don't see how I could have done that and survived. Each thing had it's purpose at the time and none of them appear to have been things that would have lasted in the long run.

So, for those reasons, I feel that a business that will not try new things is doomed to fail. I've known people who have seen the end of their business approaching like a freight train and still refused to give it up or even get out of the way. I've also known people who had businesses that appeared to be doomed because of the "big box" stores, or some other competitor, yet, they continue to thrive today because they stuck with it, tried new things, changed with the times, and made a difference in the lives of their customers.

Trying something new is not always an easy thing to do. Change is hard. The longer you've done something one way, the harder it is to change the way you do it. And people find change even harder to do than businesses. But change is one of the life-bloods of a company. You have to be ready to change when buying habits or products change.

Some people have sold XYZ for so long that they want to continue to stock it because it has always been a great product. But if the new YZA comes out that is better, cheaper, and more in demand, you have to dump the old products and get the new ones. And you can't just let the old products sit there. You have to clean house.

One of my mentors once told me that if a product didn't sell, he'd mark it down. If it still didn't sell, he'd put it on an end-cap so people could see it. If it still didn't sell, he'd mark it down and put it in the aisle where they'd have to trip over it. And if it STILL didn't sell, he'd mark them down to a nickel to get rid of them. The point? Don't keep old inventory that nobody wants. It takes up space and costs you money from lost opportunity on newer products.

Sometimes a new thing is a product. Sometimes, it is a new way of providing service or other benefits to your customers. It can be something as simple as having each employee thank each customer they see leaving the store. Chik-Fil-A has developed an amazing following just by using thankful and graceful wording when helping customers. Unfortunately, that's something "new" these days. It should have been part of every business all along.

For me, the new things have varied from services my company offered, to creating new products and manufacturing them, to going into different types of businesses and trying new sales channels. Right now, I manufacture a number of items, sell on websites, eBay, Amazon, consult for a few companies, write software, and write books. In addition to that, I am the VP of sales for a company that manufactures supplies for 3D Printers. Yes, all at once. I've been in business for myself since 1996 and had side gigs since the mid 1980's. I'm a rare bird as it were.

Why do I do all these things? To make ends meet. Because I can. Because I love it. Because I'm creative. Because I'm looking for that one thing that I absolutely love to do and can do well. Because I'm an entrepreneur. Because I am my own boss and work from home.

Keep trying new things. You never know where it will lead.

Chapter 17
Jump Ship When Times are Rough

When things started looking bad for our family business, I went to talk with my mentor. I explained that I had a business degree and that with the business failing, I wondered if I should start looking for another job. After all, bringing a business to its knees from the inside is not a really fun thing to do. I wasn't sure if I had what it took to watch it go down, or if I wanted to. I was also concerned about what I would do to make a living for my family after it did go down.

My mentor thought for a bit and then told me that I certainly could go out and find another job. It may be the safe thing to do. And it may be the best way to take care of my family. But he also told me "If you stay... and work through this. You will probably be more prepared to never let this happen to you again." It was great advice.

I stayed... for a while. During this time, my Dad and I figured out how we could spin the computer store off into its own business and keep the most successful part of what we had going. We managed to do just that and operate it for almost five more years before selling it. During all this time, I learned lessons. I learned how to separate a good business from one that was breathing its last breaths. I learned how to start up a new business on a shoestring and make it a success, and grow it over a four-year period. I learned valuable lessons about dealing with employees.

My undergraduate degree in business hardly prepared me to be a success in a business. It merely touched the edges of what I needed to know and learn. Being a part of a business that thrived and grew and had a lot of employees taught me much more. Having my own business, being the person sitting at the desk where the buck stops, taught me even more. Having it reach a point where I could no longer keep it going was an extremely difficult learning experience. But, I'm better for it.

This is one of the short and sweet lessons. When things get tough, you can always jump ship and go somewhere else "safe." That may be the right thing for you depending on where you are in life and what you and your family need. But if you stay... if you follow through the tough times... if you persevere through the hardest things you'll ever do in business... you'll learn lessons that others will only dream of learning.

I hope you never have to be in a business that fails. If you avoid a lot of these pitfalls I am writing about, maybe you won't. But if you are in one. Make the best of it. If the ship is sinking, save all you can. Help employees find jobs. Liquidate inventory to pay bills. Have a going out of business sale where you make a little less on products, but keep them coming in until the sale is over so you can make a little extra profit to pay off creditors. Talk with your banker and keep them informed. Avoid bankruptcy if you can and try to pay off all your suppliers without having to settle for smaller payment. Show people what you're made of. Let people remember that you were honest, dependable, and helped others right up to the end of the business.

Then, look for something new and start a new business with the newly acquired knowledge you have and make it a big success.

Chapter 18
Stay out of reach of your customers

When we were selling Stereo systems and audio, one of our lines was Pioneer. Pioneer used Representative Firms to promote their products and to work with individual dealers. So, we had a man who lived in the next state over who would come to see us once or twice a year and go over our big orders for the fall or the new line of products.

He was a nice guy and I really liked working with him. Once, when I was in his hometown, I told him I would be over there and he suggested I come by his office. His office was in the basement of his home. So, I pictured a 3-bedroom ranch home with a full basement, somewhat finished, and his office and some shelves for the literature he had to keep and went to see him.

As I approached his home, I noticed that this was quite a nice neighborhood. In fact, it was one of the nicest neighborhoods I'd been in. Then when I found his address, there was a gate with a driveway that led up the side of a hill so steep that it had switch-back hairpin turns on the way up. When I arrived at the top, I saw a very large and beautiful home hidden in the woods at the top of a private hill in one of the largest cities in the Southeast. Wow. I was impressed.

In the tour of his house, we saw a little of the main floor and then down to the basement. As you can imagine, this was no shabby paneled basement with dirt floors. It was a really nice office. With an office for him, one for his secretary, a small room for shipping and receiving literature and product samples, and storage.

As we toured, he commented, "Yeah, this is the house Pioneer built," indicating that it was his commissions that made all this possible. We had a nice visit and I left quite impressed and wondering what I was doing where I was.

Shouldn't I become a Manufacturer's Representative? After all, if there's that kind of money in it, surely there's room for more.

On the way home, I came up with my idea. Since I was into computers and it was a new field, there must be many companies looking for reps that would love to have me represent their products. So, I came up with MicroRep Sales. "Representing Manufacturers to the Micro-Computer Industry." And, of course, I made up some business cards.

I was still working for the family business, but with Dad's approval, I began to try to build the business. I rented a small office, got a telephone line installed (there were no cell phones in the mid 1980's), started calling some companies and even got hired over the phone to represent a floppy disc company for whom I had sold a lot of product. I added one or two more lines and then took a trip to nearby cities to offer my wares. I spent money on phones, rent, travel, lodging, gas, and more. I sold a few items, but it just didn't seem to be working. I couldn't figure out why it wasn't working.

During all this time, I continued to work at the family business during most days, only travelling occasionally. And I'd "man the phones" at the office late afternoons and evening. But the sales just didn't cover the expenses. So, I closed it down.

It was during the time that I was moving my furniture out of the office that someone in the office building saw me moving the desk out to the truck. She stopped me and asked "Are you the person who's been renting that office?" "Yes" I replied. She then said, "Well, we've been wondering whose office that was. The phone rings off the hook! It rings off and on all day!"

And here's the really sad part. Our family business also sold **telephone answering machines!** Had I just installed an answering machine (this was pre-voicemail), I may have been able to sell more and make it work. But I didn't see the problem until it was too late.

Since that time, I've been involved in several businesses and several websites. To this day, it amazes me when I try to contact someone from their website only to find that there is no way to communicate with them! Sometimes, there's not even a phone number or an email address. Others go a little further and put up a form where you can leave them a message. But I think most people think those things go into a trash can somewhere.

Do yourself a favor. Be available. Put your cell phone right on the website, in your emails, on your business cards. Give your email out openly. Yes, you'll be added to some mailing lists, so what? You'll be available to your customers and they will not believe how well they are treated when you actually respond to them. It's not hard to be special in today's world. All you have to do is be nice and available. Customers love it.

I'm in a business right now with others and we had a competitor who really didn't understand the business or how to make the products. But he did anyway. He was one of the first in the business, so he had a big following. But he started making mistakes and having issues. The first thing he did was make sure no one could contact him. Even early on, he didn't have his phone number posted, and there was no email address. He took orders on the website, but if he couldn't deliver or had an issue, he just ignored it.

As you can imagine, this snowballed and eventually, he had so many complaints with the Better Business Bureau that he had to close down his site and change his name. But the BBB saw right through it and attached the complaints to the new business as well.

This man could have saved his business and kept his customers if he had only communicated with them and treated them with respect and honesty. Instead, I'm not sure he even has a business anymore.

Our similar business has our email on every page next to our phone number. We have a chat that we answer personally during business hours and a "contact us" form if you want to leave a question. And guess what? We read all of them every day and respond to any one that leaves their email for us to get in touch with them. The result? We can't make the product fast enough right now.

Communicate with your customers. Let them find you. Be nice when they call. Be available. You'll stand out in the crowd as someone really special.

Chapter 19
Don't stand behind your products

If you really want to kill your business, sell shoddy merchandise and then leave your customers to suffer through them alone. It's one of the fastest ways to ruin a business.

Along the way, I've learned so many things about selling and products. So many that I couldn't begin to list them all. But a few of them made a big difference for me, and the business. For instance, if you really want to be successful, choose a product or service that has real value. Not just a high price, a real value. Something that is worth much more than the price to the customer. Often this is something that no one else offers, or is willing to do or sell. Sometimes, you just find the right product and it meets the needs of the masses and is priced reasonably. And if it holds up to wear and tear, then it's a real diamond of a product!

When I ran an Apple Dealership, I was surprised when they "forced" us to buy parts to repair all their products. They even "made" us attend service training! How dare they try to run our business! Of course, they already knew that the secret to keeping customers is to make sure they have good operational products. You can't keep a customer happy whose product is broken and sitting on a shelf waiting for parts.

Apple knew this so well that they covered FEDEX shipping both ways for any warranty part. They understood that making the customer happy, as soon as possible, and letting them know that both the dealer and the company stood behind the products was paramount for success. Of course, we learned the same thing very quickly. Even in our family business, we operated a full service department and could fix nearly anything we sold. We sent people to training on everything from copiers to video recorders and cameras. Customers expect it. If you sell a product, you should expect to take care of the customers, too!

Nowadays, (do they even say "nowadays" nowadays?) many manufacturers just replace any item that fails. Bad television, we'll just give you a new one. iPhone doesn't work? We'll replace it. And you can buy your own warranty to cover almost anything including being an idiot. But what people really want... is to have someone they can turn to that will "take care of it for them." You need to be that person.

A few years ago, I developed a product and started selling it. The product was supposed to be cleaned every month in a solution of water and ammonia. After I'd been selling them about four or five months, I discovered that the glue I used on them was **water soluble!** What a mistake! That meant I had sold over 1000 of this item and they were ALL BAD! It was a nightmare for me.

First, I took stock and figured out just how bad it was. Then, I started to dig my way out of the situation. I found the right glue and fixed the manufacturing problem as soon as possible. Next, I recalled all the product that was "on the shelf" by recalling it all from Amazon. Finally, I tried to send an email to every customer that bought one of the defective units and offered them a free replacement for every one they had purchased. I didn't make much on them in the first place, and this meant I was going to lose a lot of money on the "fix" for the problem.

It did not matter whether it was profitable. It did not matter that it was a lot of work for me. It did not matter that I had to manually disassemble 100's of the products to try and rebuild them to save some of the money I was losing. What mattered was that I tried to take care of my customers. They had trusted me and I had failed them. Was it intentional? No, of course not. Did they care whether I meant to do it or not? Probably not. All they wanted was a good product that worked as advertised. When it didn't, all they really wanted was someone to address the problem and solve it for them.

Why did I go to the trouble? It may have been less expensive to just start making good ones and replace only the ones who contacted me with a complaint. The reason I did all that was to preserve my reputation. Not just on Amazon (and that was a big part of it), but I wanted everyone who ever did business with me to know that I was honest, dependable, and would make things right. There's no other correct response to a mistake like that. You must take care of the customers.

I've had other products that I've manufactured, made on a 3D Printer, or sold that didn't quite work right or fit right or whatever over the years. When it was brought to my attention, I either fixed it or stopped selling the product.

So, what has this gained me? Well, hopefully a good reputation as I have said. It has also helped others to know that I support what I sell. And when someone has a problem with a product, I try to let them know right up front that I'll take care of it. As a result, I've had an online business since 1994 or 1995 with excellent ratings. Both Amazon and eBay list me as a great seller and I have great feedback on almost all my sales. That's worth a lot.

Years ago, I worked for my uncle in one of the family business's Hi-Fi Stereo Shops. He was instructing me on how to handle an irate customer. You know, the kind that brings in their broken item and wants to throw it at you. They come in all puffed up, assuming that you won't help them. That you'll somehow say it is out of warranty, or tell them it's because of abuse. You can see them as they come through the door and you want to just run and hide.

Well he gave me the best advice for taking care of a customer that I have ever received. He said the first thing you need to do is decide to LOVE that person. Because when you love someone, you do things for them, for their good, and expect nothing in return. But just deciding to love someone is not going to stop their rampage. So, he told me the next secret.

When they approach all mad and huffing and puffing trying to tell you what you're going to do for them, just quietly interrupt them and say "Excuse me. Before you get started, I want you to know that we are going to do whatever you think is fair. Will that be ok with you?" This really takes them by surprise, because, in most people's experience, NOBODY does that! It allows them to stop and think, and maybe they'll be in shock a little. But they will be instantly disarmed.

Once they hear you say that you are really going to help them, they back down. They can explain the problem. They can talk with you, and you can talk with them. You can address the issue and fix the problem. Most of the time, they don't really need much help; they just want someone to fix the problem and expected you to refuse them the service.

When you stand behind your problems, and yes, even love your customers, you will have them singing your praises to everyone they know. They'll send all their friends to you and become your best advertisements.

Chapter 20
Treat Your Customers Like Enemies

I have already talked about how to treat customers throughout this book. But it is amazing to me how some people really miss this. I actually worked for a man in retail for a while. I saw this man work with a customer to sell him a computer system. From afar, I saw him work with him, get him interested, start negotiating, and then all but pistol-whip him into a frenzy. He started arguing with the man and causing the customer to get mad and nearly stomp out the door. Then, at the last minute, he backed down a little and let the customer buy the computer. I could not believe what I had just witnessed.

After the customer left, I asked him what he was doing? His reply was almost disgusting. He said that he believed that before you could negotiate with a customer, you had to have the upper hand. Whatever it took to get there, that's what you had to do. So, he felt that he had to irritate the customer until he had the upper hand, and only then, could he negotiate and become some sort of "hero." It was ridiculous.

Customers are not our enemies. They should be our friends. We cannot survive without customers and we need every customer we can get. Repeating customers are the best! They keep on coming back and buying more from us. What more could you ask of someone?

When I was in Junior High School, the family business had starting selling school supplies. And it was in the early 1970's when Monogramming was getting big for the first time. People were monogramming *everything!* Even their cars! You'd see big silver or gold stick-on letters on the side panels of landau roofs and down the sides of the doors. Everything was being engraved, too. Signet rings, charms, bracelets, every kind of jewelry. And this went on to even books and notebooks.

If you could get your initials on something, that suddenly made it cool.

In our store, we sold peel and stick vinyl letters. So, naturally, I saw the opportunity. I either bought a set or just took it and told my mother (we had all the school supplies we needed during those years!). And then, I took them to school. I was selling the letters about ¾" tall for a nickel each. So, you could have your initials on something for only 15¢! What a deal. I was doing well, and my friends were buying. Until, someone saw my package of letters.

Right there on the package was the price tag. I think the whole set was probably about $1.79 for about 10 sets of letters and some punctuation marks. So, probably about 300 characters. One of my smart-aleck friends started doing some math and figured out that I only had about 2¢ in each letter and was selling them for more than double the cost. Then, they exaggerated and started telling people I was making 1000% profit. I was very embarrassed!

That afternoon, I went to Dad and told him what happened. And that I had been embarrassed about making money on what I sold to my friends. He came back to me with some consolation and then gave me one of the "Wizbits" I wrote about in Wizbits from Dad: "Carl, you have to make money off your friends... because your enemies won't buy from you."

Now, **_that's_** some sage advice! We must make friends of our customers. Enemies won't come back. They won't tell their friends. They won't recommend your business. Only friends will do that for you. So, whenever we work with a customer, we need to remember that if they're not already a friend, we need to turn them into one.

What does this look like in business? Well, just like this book, you can tell what it looks like by looking at what it does NOT look like. Here are some examples:

Friends don't gouge friends on pricing. There is nothing wrong with making a profit. We must make a profit in order to stay in business so that we can help our friends in the future. Profit is good! It is not a four-letter word like "loss," it's a FIVE letter word, and a good one! Profit is our friend. But when supply is low, and you have some of the product, it's ok to mark it up a little. Supply and demand control pricing... to an extent. But if there has been a hurricane and you have the only gas for miles, it's not right to start charging $10 a gallon. That's gouging.

Friends don't forget their friends. How frustrating is it for you to enter a store that you've shopped in for years, calling the owner by name, and he has no idea what your name is? When I had a computer store, I knew most of my customers by names. And the names of their children! And I knew what computer they had, how much memory it had in it, what kind of printer they had, and when they were going to run out of ink! Well, most of that, anyway. The thing is, get to KNOW your customers. Learn about them and their likes and dislikes in the area in which you serve them.

Friends don't recommend purchases that their friends don't need. One of the best things about selling is learning that you're not pushing anything on anybody when you do it right. You're simply assisting people to get the things they want and need. As long as you're doing that, you are "taking care" of your customers. Customers love to be "taken care of." They long for someone they can trust who will listen to them, determine their needs, and then recommend the solution. That is what friends do.

Friends don't avoid their friends. Some of you may remember the TV show "Cheers" where "everyone knows your name." When Norm walked into the bar, everyone in the bar said "Norm!" and he'd reply with some cute response. We all love to hear our names. When you see a customer, whether it is in your business, while you are out at lunch, or at the ballpark, go up to them and shake their hand, call them by name, and ask how they're doing. Then, they'll know you care. And when they speak... really listen.

Want to really kill your business? Treat your customers like you hate them. That'll do it.

Become a contributor to the next 20 Ways book!

Go to www.cp3books.com and look for your chance to enter your lesson learned and you'll have a chance to be included in the next version. Why not share your valuable insight with other entrepreneurs! Those chosen will receive a free copy of the next book when published and be credited for their contribution.